REALLY EASY GUITAR

THE DOORS

22 SONGS WITH CHORDS, LYRICS & BASIC TAB

ISBN 978-1-5400-9253-3

Visit Hal Leonard Online at
www.halleonard.com

Contact us:
Hal Leonard
7777 West Bluemound Road
Milwaukee, WI 53213
Email: info@halleonard.com

In Europe, contact:
Hal Leonard Europe Limited
42 Wigmore Street
Marylebone, London, W1U 2RN
Email: info@halleonardeurope.com

In Australia, contact:
Hal Leonard Australia Pty. Ltd.
4 Lentara Court
Cheltenham, Victoria, 3192 Australia
Email: info@halleonard.com.au

GUITAR NOTATION LEGEND

Chord Diagrams

CHORD DIAGRAMS graphically represent the guitar fretboard to show correct chord fingerings.

- The letter above the diagram tells the name of the chord.
- The top, bold horizontal line represents the nut of the guitar. Each thin horizontal line represents a fret. Each vertical line represents a string; the low E string is on the far left and the high E string is on the far right.
- A dot shows where to put your fret-hand finger and the number at the bottom of the diagram tells which finger to use.
- The "O" above the string means play it open, while an "X" means don't play the string.

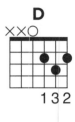

Tablature

TABLATURE graphically represents the guitar fingerboard. Each horizontal line represents a string, and each number represents a fret.

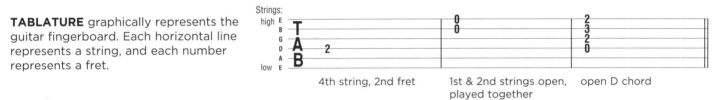

4th string, 2nd fret   1st & 2nd strings open, played together   open D chord

Definitions for Special Guitar Notation

HAMMER-ON: Strike the first (lower) note with one finger, then sound the higher note (on the same string) with another finger by fretting it without picking.

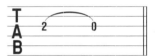

PULL-OFF: Place both fingers on the notes to be sounded. Strike the first note and without picking, pull the finger off to sound the second (lower) note.

LEGATO SLIDE: Strike the first note and then slide the same fret-hand finger up or down to the second note. The second note is not struck.

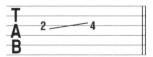

SHIFT SLIDE: Same as legato slide, except the second note is struck.

Additional Musical Definitions

N.C.   • No chord. Instrument is silent.

    • Repeat measures between signs.

Been Down So Long

Words & Music by The Doors

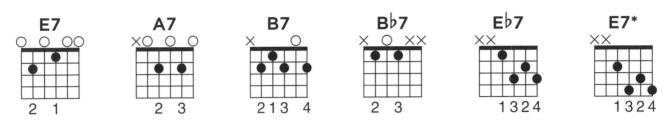

VERSE 1

Moderately

      E7
Well, I been down so God damn long that it looks like up to me.

      A7   **E7**
Well, I been down so very damn long that it looks like up to me.

    B7   **Bb7** **A7** **N.C.**   **E7**
Yeah, why don't one you people   come on and set me free?

VERSE 2

      E7
I said, "Warden, warden, warden, won't you break your lock and key?"

    A7   **E7**
I said, "Warden, warden, warden, won't you break your lock and key?"

    B7   **Bb7** **A7** **N.C.**   **E7**
Yeah, come along here, mister,   come on and let the poor boy be.

GUITAR SOLO 1

```
||: E7              |              |              |          :||

||: A7              |      :|||: E7       |              :||

    B7              |      Bb7 | A7   N.C.        |              |

    E7              |              |              ||
```

VERSE 3

E7
Baby, baby, baby, won't you get down on your knee?

A7   **E7**
Baby, baby, baby, won't you get down on your knee?

B7   **Bb7** **A7** **N.C.**   **E7**
Come on, little darlin',   come on and give your love to me. Oh, yeah.

GUITAR SOLO 2

‖: A7 | :‖: E7 | :‖

B7 | B♭7 | A7 | |

E7 | | | ‖

Well, I been

VERSE 4

E7
down so God damn long that it looks like up to me.

    A7   E7
Well, I been down so very damn long that it looks like up to me.

    B7   B♭7 A7 N.C.   A7 N.C.   A7 N.C.   A7 N.C.
Yeah, why don't one you people   come on,   come on,   come on   and set me

E7   E♭7 E7*
free?!

Break on Through
(To the Other Side)

Words & Music by The Doors

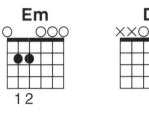

INTRO

Moderately fast

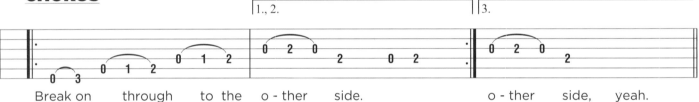

You know the

VERSE 1

Em
day destroys the night, night divides the day.

D
Tried to run, tried to hide.

CHORUS

1., 2.   3.

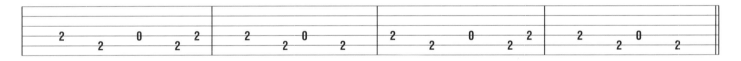

Break on   through   to the   o - ther   side.   o - ther   side,   yeah.

INTERLUDE

We

VERSE 2

Em
chased our pleasures here, dug our treasures there.

D
Can't you still recall, time we cried?

CHORUS

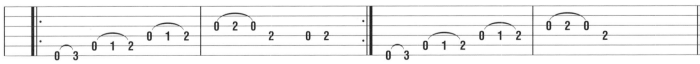

Break on   through to the o - ther side.

KEYBOARD SOLO

Play 4 times

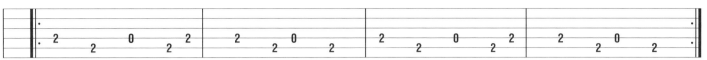

INTERLUDE 1

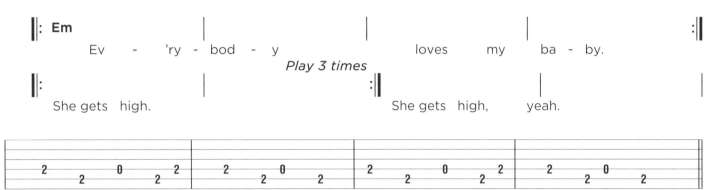

Em

Ev - 'ry - bod - y   loves   my   ba - by.

Play 3 times

She gets high.   She gets high,   yeah.

I found an

VERSE 3

Em
island in your arms, country in your eyes.

D
Arms that chained us. Eyes that lied.

CHORUS

Play 3 times   *Play 3 times*

Break on through {1., 2. to the o - ther side.
              { 3. oh!   Oh,   *yeah! }
                                  *1st time only

VERSE 4

Em
Made the scene, week to week, day to day, hour to hour.

D
Gate is straight, deep and wide.

OUTRO - CHORUS

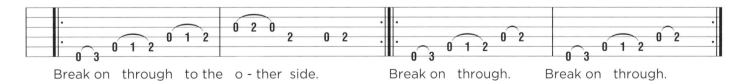

Break on through to the o - ther side.   Break on through.   Break on through.

Em
Yeah, yeah, yeah, yeah, yeah, yeah, yeah, yeah, yeah.

The Changeling

Words & Music by The Doors

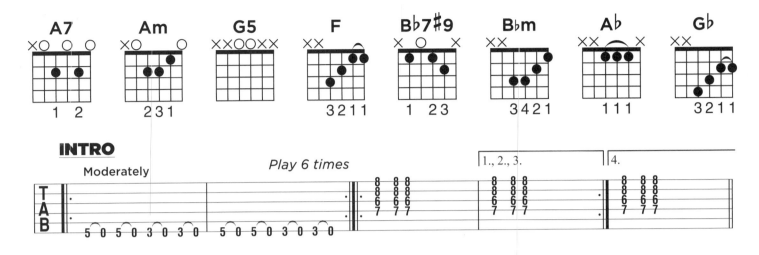

INTRO

Moderately   *Play 6 times*

VERSE 1

A7

I live   uptown, I live downtown, I live all around.

I had money, I had none; I had money, I had none; But I

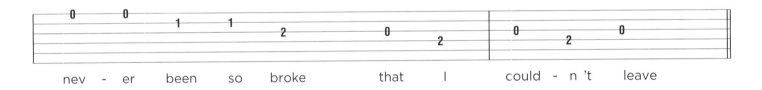

nev - er   been   so   broke   that   I   could - n't   leave

CHORUS 1

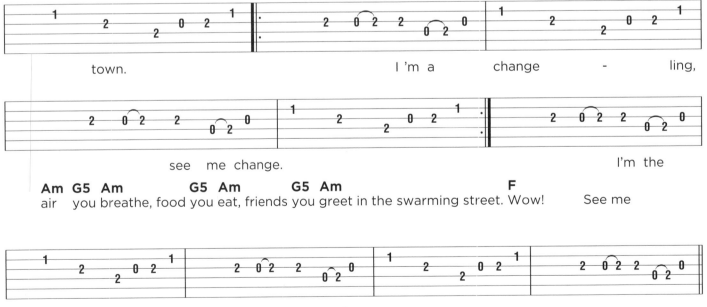

town.   I'm a   change - ling,

see me change.   I'm the

Am G5 Am   G5 Am   G5 Am   F

air you breathe, food you eat, friends you greet in the swarming street. Wow!   See me

change,   see me change.

INTERLUDE

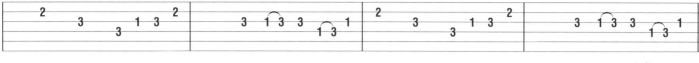

I live

VERSE 2

Bb7#9

uptown, I live downtown, I live all around.

I had money, I had none; I had money, I had none; But I

nev - er   been   so   broke   that   I   could - n 't   leave

GUITAR SOLO

Bbm

town.

Play 7 times

Well, I'm the

OUTRO-CHORUS

Bbm Ab Bbm   Ab Bbm   Ab Bbm   Gb
air   you breathe, food you eat, friends you greet in the swarming street. Wow!   You got to see me

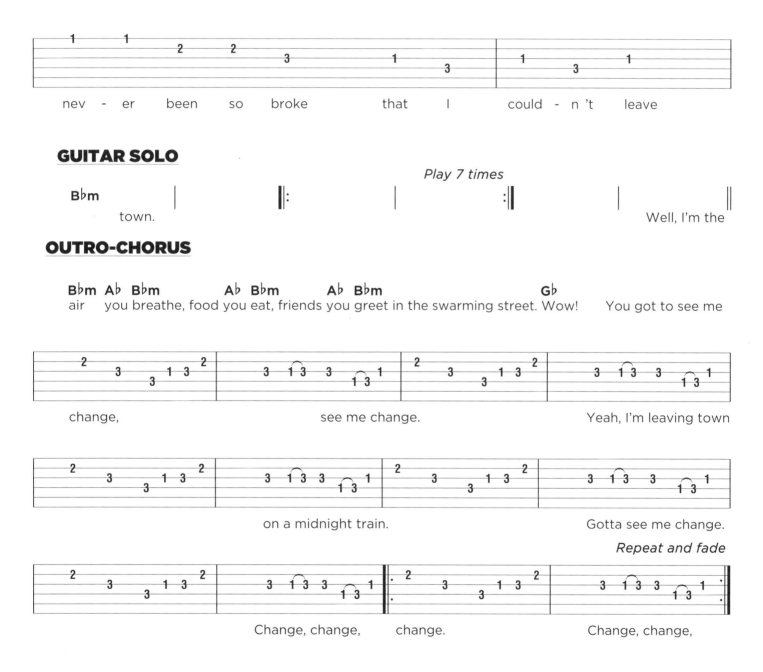

change,   see me change.   Yeah, I'm leaving town

on a midnight train.   Gotta see me change.

Repeat and fade

Change, change,   change.   Change, change,

Five to One

Words & Music by The Doors

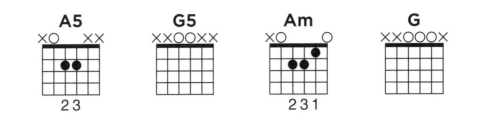

INTRO

Moderately

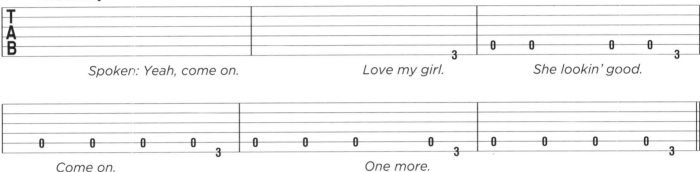

Spoken: Yeah, come on.   *Love my girl.*   *She lookin' good.*

Come on.   *One more.*

VERSE 1

A5   G5 A5   G5
Five to one, baby,   one in five.

A5   G5 A5   G5
No one here gets   out alive, now.

A5   G5 A5   G5
You get yours, baby,   I'll get mine.

A5   G5 Am   G5 Am   G5 Am   G
Gonna make it, baby,   if we try.   The

VERSE 2

Am   G Am   G
old get old and the   young get stronger.

Am   G Am   G
May take a week and it   may take longer.

Am   G Am   G
They got the guns but   we got the numbers.

Am N.C.   Am
Gonna win, yeah, we're takin' over. Come on!

GUITAR SOLO

Play 4 times

‖: Am   G | Am   G :‖ Am N.C.   G ‖

VERSE 3

A5 N.C.   G5 A5   G5
Your ballroom days are over, baby.

A5 N.C.   G5 A5   G5
Night is drawing near.

A5 N.C.   G5 A5   G5
Shadows of the   evening

A5 N.C.   G5 A5   G5
crawl across the years.

A5 N.C. G5   A5   G5 A5 N.C.   G5
You walk across the floor with a   flower in your hand;

A5   G5 A5 N.C.   G5
Try'na tell me no one   understands.

A5   G5 A5   N.C.   G5
Trade in your hours for a   handful of dimes.

A5 N.C.   G5
Gonna make it, baby, in our own prime.

A5 N.C.   G5
Get together one more time.

A5 N.C.   G5
Get together one more time.

A5 N.C.   G5
Get together one more time.

A5
Get together one more time.

OUTRO

Play 7 times

‖: Am   G | Am   G :‖
*Get to - ge - ther   one more   time.
*background vocals, lead vocal ad lib.

Am N.C. | |
Get to - ge - ther   one more   time.

‖: | :‖
Get to - ge - ther   one more   time.

                              | G |
Get to - ge - ther   one more   time.

Repeat and fade

‖: Am   G | Am   G ‖
Get to - ge - ther   one more   time.

Hello, I Love You

Words & Music by The Doors

INTRO

Moderately

Hel -

CHORUS 1

```
A G           A
lo, I love you, won't you tell me your name?

         G         A
Hello, I love you, let me jump in your game.

         G         A
Hello, I love you, won't you tell me your name?

         G         A
Hello, I love you, let me jump in your game.
```

VERSE 1

```
    A  G    A  G
She's walking down the street,

A    G    A    G
blind to ev'ry eye she meets.

    A    G   A   G
Do you think you'll be the guy

    A    G    A    G
to make the queen of the angels sigh?
```

CHORUS 2

```
    A G           A
Hello, I love you, won't you tell me your name?

    G         A
Hello, I love you, let me jump in your game.

    G         A
Hello, I love you, won't you tell me your name?

    G         A
Hello, I love you, let me jump in your game.
```

VERSE 2

      A   G   A   G
She holds her head so high,

        A   G   A G
like a statue in the sky.

       A   G   A   G
Her arms are wicked and her legs are long.

          A   G   A   G   A N.C.
When she moves my brain screams out this song.

VERSE 3

B♭   A♭   B♭   A♭
Sidewalk crouches at her feet,

     B♭   A♭   B♭   A♭
like a dog that begs for something sweet.

       B♭   A♭   B♭   A♭
Do you hope to make her see you, fool?

       B♭   A♭   B♭   A♭
Do you hope to pluck this dusky jewel? Hel -

OUTRO

Repeat and fade

B♭   A♭ | B♭   A♭   ‖: B♭   A♭ | B♭   A♭   :‖
lo!   Hello!   Hello!   Hello!   Hello!

Indian Summer

(Morrison/Krieger)

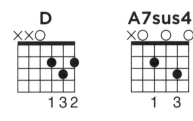

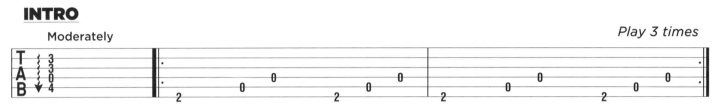

INTRO

Moderately

Play 3 times

VERSE 1

D
I love you the best, better than all the rest.

I love you the best, better than all the rest

CHORUS 1

A7sus4   **D**
that I meet in the summer,

A7sus4   **D**
Indian   summer.

GUITAR SOLO

D

CHORUS 2

A7sus4   **D**
That I meet in the summer,

A7sus4   **D**
Indian   summer.

OUTRO

D
I love you the best, better than all the rest.

L.A. Woman

Words & Music by The Doors

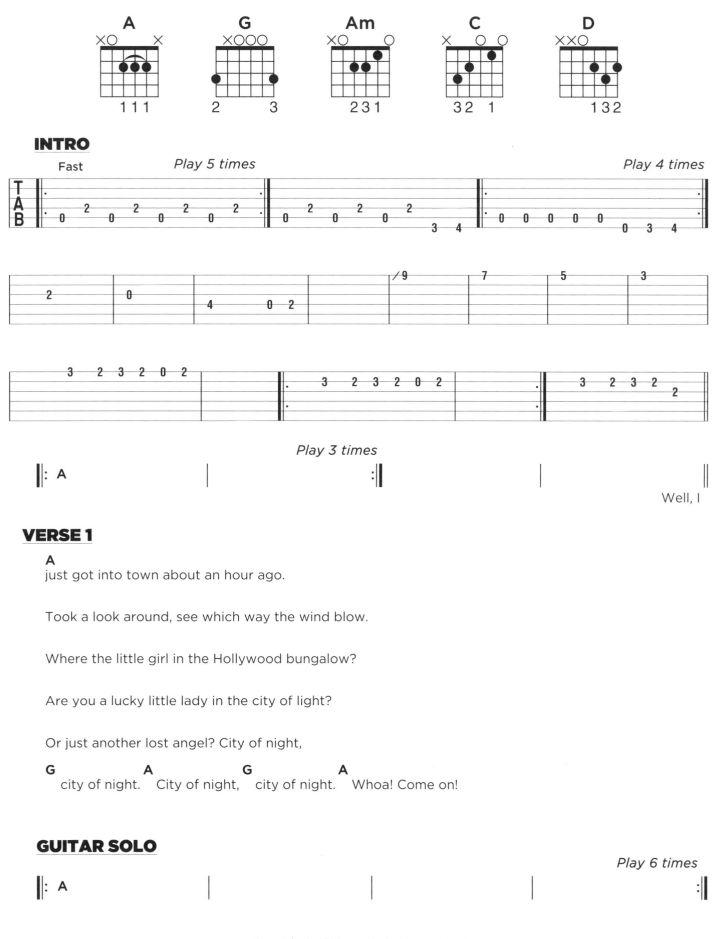

INTRO

Fast   *Play 5 times*   *Play 4 times*

Play 3 times

|: A | :| | |

Well, I

VERSE 1

A
just got into town about an hour ago.

Took a look around, see which way the wind blow.

Where the little girl in the Hollywood bungalow?

Are you a lucky little lady in the city of light?

Or just another lost angel? City of night,

G   **A**   **G**   **A**
city of night.   City of night,   city of night.   Whoa! Come on!

GUITAR SOLO

Play 6 times

|: A | | | :|

VERSE 2

A
L. A. woman, L. A. woman.

L. A. woman Sunday afternoon.

L. A. woman Sunday afternoon.

L. A. woman Sunday afternoon, drive through your suburbs into your

G   **A**   **G**   **A**
blues. Into your blues. Yeah! Into your blue, blue, blue, into your blues. Oh,

PIANO SOLO

Play 7 times

A | ‖: | :‖
yeah!

INTERLUDE 1

Play 3 times

‖: A   G | A   G   :‖ A   G | A   G   ‖

BRIDGE

A   G   A G A G A G   A   G   A G A G A G
see your   hair is burning;   hills are   filled with fire.

      A   G   A   G A G A   G   G   A G A G A G
If they say I   never loved you,   you know they   are a li - ar.

A   G   A G A G A G   G   A G A G A G
Driving   down your freeway,   midnight   alleys roam.

A   **G   A   G   A**
Cops in cars, the topless bars, never saw a woman so alone, so alone.   So alone, so alone.

Motel money, murder madness,

change the mood from glad to sadness.

INTERLUDE 2

Half-time   *Play 5 times*

‖: **Am** | :‖ | |

                                          Mister

   C Am   **C Am**   **C Am**   **C Am**
Mojo ris - in'.   Mister Mojo ris - in'.   Mister Mojo ris - in'.   Mister Mojo ris - in'.

                                         slowly accel.
   C Am   **C Am**   **C Am**   **C Am**
Gotta keep on ris - in'.   Mister Mojo ris - in'.   Mister Mojo ris - in'.   Mojo ris - in'.

   C Am   **C Am**   **C Am**   **C Am**
Got my Mojo ris - in'.   Mister Mojo ris - in'.   Gotta keep on ris - in'.   Ridin', rid - in'.

    C Am   **C Am**   **C Am**   **C Am**
Gone ridin', rid - in'.   I'm goin' ridin', rid - in'.   I got to ridin', rid - in'.   Well, ridin', rid - in'.   I gotta,

INTERLUDE 2

A tempo I

C | | | | | |
wooo,   yeah,   right!   Oh!   Yeah!

D | | | | | |

A | | | | | ‖
                                                                 Well, I...

REPEAT VERSE 1

PIANO SOLO

‖: **A** | | | | | :‖

OUTRO

A
L. A. woman, L. A. woman

L. A. woman, you're my woman.

My little L. A. woman, yeah, my L. A. woman.

Fade out

'Ay, 'ay, come on, come on, L. A. woman come on.

Light My Fire

Words & Music by The Doors

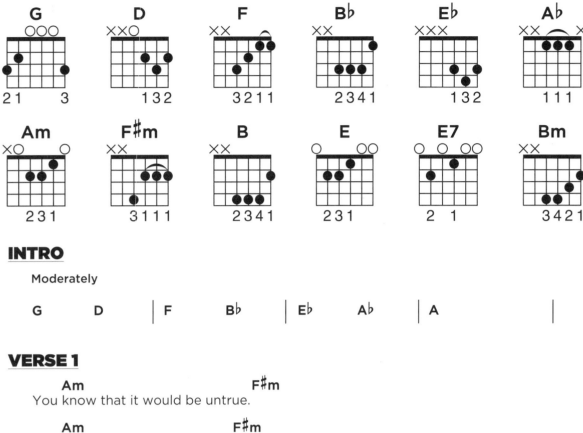

INTRO

Moderately

| G | D | | F | Bb | | Eb | Ab | | A | | | | |

VERSE 1

      Am   F#m
You know that it would be untrue.

      Am   F#m
You know that I would be a liar

Am   F#m
if I was to say to you,

Am   F#m
girl, we couldn't get much higher.

CHORUS 1

G   A   D
Come on, baby, light my fire.

G   A   D   B
Come on, baby, light my fire.

G   D   E   E7
Try to set the night on   fire.   *(Yeah!)

                 *2nd and 3rd time only

VERSE 2

      Am   F#m
The time to hesitate is through.

      Am   F#m
No time to wallow in the mire.

Am   F#m
Try now we can only lose,

        Am   F#m
and our love become a funeral pyre.

REPEAT CHORUS 1

ORGAN SOLO

Play 35 times

‖: Am   Bm | Am   Bm   :‖

GUITAR SOLO

Play 35 times

‖: Am   Bm | Am   Bm   :‖

INTERLUDE

G   D | F   B♭ | E♭   A♭ | A | ‖

                                                               The

REPEAT VERSE 2

REPEAT CHORUS 1

REPEAT VERSE 1

CHORUS 2

G   A   D
Come on, baby, light my fire.

G   A   D
Come on, baby, light my fire.

F   C   D
Try to set the night on fire.

F   C   D
Try to set the night on fire.

F   C   D
Try to set the night on fire.

F   C   D
Try to set the night on fire!

OUTRO

G   D | F   B♭ | E♭   A♭ | A | ‖

Love Her Madly

Words & Music by The Doors

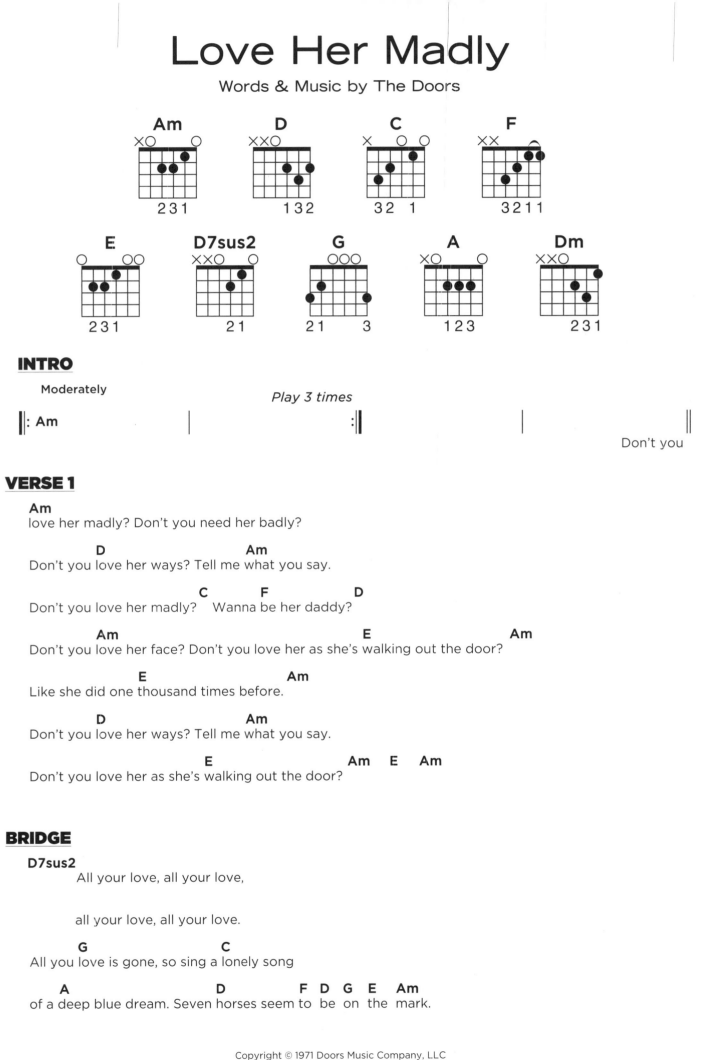

INTRO

Moderately

Play 3 times

‖: Am | | :‖ | ‖

Don't you

VERSE 1

Am
love her madly? Don't you need her badly?

D   Am
Don't you love her ways? Tell me what you say.

                    C   F   D
Don't you love her madly?   Wanna be her daddy?

         Am   E   Am
Don't you love her face? Don't you love her as she's walking out the door?

         E   Am
Like she did one thousand times before.

         D   Am
Don't you love her ways? Tell me what you say.

                              E   Am E Am
Don't you love her as she's walking out the door?

BRIDGE

D7sus2
      All your love, all your love,

      all your love, all your love.

      G   C
All you love is gone, so sing a lonely song

      A   D   F D G E Am
of a deep blue dream. Seven horses seem to be on the mark.

KEYBOARD SOLO

‖: Am | | | :‖

VERSE 2

Am   C   F   D
   Yeah,   don't you love her?

          Am   E   Am E Am
Don't you love her as she's walking out the door?

REPEAT BRIDGE

GUITAR SOLO

Am | | | |

Dm | | Am | |

          | C | F | D |

Am | | | ‖

                                         Well, don't you

OUTRO

Am
love her madly? Don't you love her madly?

Don't you love her madly?

                                        Repeat and fade

‖: Am | | :‖

Love Me Two Times

Words & Music by The Doors

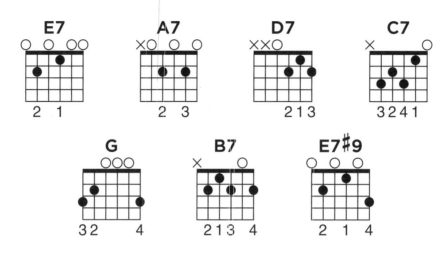

INTRO

Moderately

Play 3 times

Love me two time, ba -

VERSE 1

E7
- by. Love me twice today.

A7   **E7**
Love me two time, girl. I'm goin' away.

D7   **C7**
Love me two time, girl,   one for tomorrow, one just for today.

G   **D7 C7 B7**
Love me two times,   I'm goin' away.

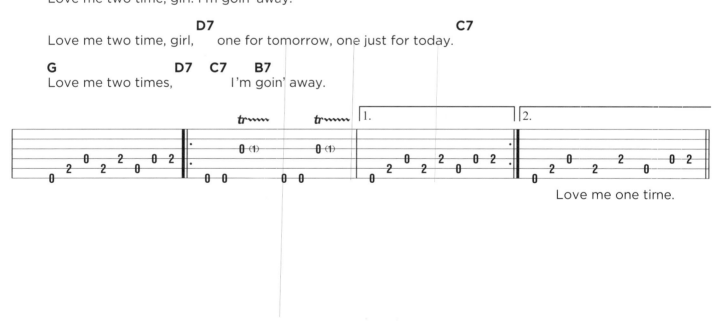

Love me one time.

VERSE 2

E7
    Could not speak.

               A7   E7
Love me one time.   Yeah, my knees got weak.

                         D7   C7
Love me two times, girl,   last me all through the week.

G   D7   C7   B7   E7♯9
Love me two times,   I'm goin' away.

G   D7   C7   B7   E7
Love me two times,   I'm goin' away.   Oh, yeah!

KEYBOARD SOLO

| E7 | | | | A7 | | E7 | | |

| G D7 | C7 B7 | E7♯9 | | | G D7 | C7 B7 | |

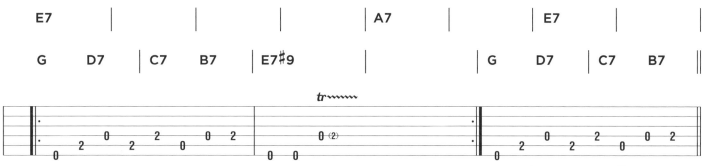

Love me one time.

VERSE 3

E7
    Could not speak.

               A7   E7
Love me one time, baby. Yeah, my knees got weak.

                       D7   C7
Love me two time, girl,   last me all through the week.

G   D7   C7   B7   E7
Love me two times,   I'm goin' away.

Love me two time, babe. Love me twice today.

               A7   E7
Love me two time, babe, 'cause I'm goin' away.

                       D7   C7
Love me two time, girl,   one for tomorrow, one just for today.

G   D7   C7   B7   E7♯9
Love me two times,   I'm goin' away.

G   D7   C7   B7   E7♯9
Love me two times,   I'm goin' away.

G   D7   C7   B7   E7♯9
Love me two times,   I'm   goin' away.

Love Street

Words & Music by The Doors

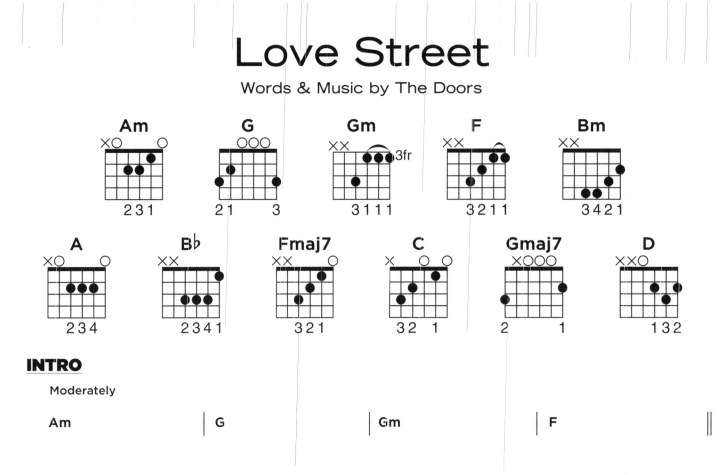

INTRO

Moderately

| Am | | G | | Gm | | F | ||

VERSE 1

Am   G   Gm   F
She lives on Love Street. Lingers long on Love Street.

Am   G   Gm   F
She has a house   and garden,   I would like to see   what happens.

Bm   A   Am   G

VERSE 2

Am   G   Gm   F
She has robes and she has monkeys,   lazy diamond studded flunkies.

Gm   Am   B♭   Fmaj7
She has wisdom and knows what to do.

Gm   Fmaj7   B♭   A
She has me and she has you.

PIANO SOLO

|: Bm | | A | | Am | | G | :|

BRIDGE

Am Bm   C   Gmaj7
She has wisdom and knows what to do.

Am Gmaj7 C G A
She has me and she has you.

VERSE 3

Am   G Gm   F
 I see you live on Love Street, there's the store where the creatures meet.

 Am   G Gm   F
I wonder what they do in there; Summer Sunday and a year.

Am   G   Gm F
 I guess I like it fine so far.

INTERLUDE

Gm | F | C | D | ‖

VERSE 4

Bm   A   Am   G
 She lives on Love Street. Lingers long on Love Street.

Bm   A   Am   G
 She has a house and garden, I would like to see what happens.

Bm   A   Am   G
 La la la la - la la la. La la la la - la la la.

                  Fade out
Bm   A   Am   G
 La la la la - la la la. La la la la - la la la.

Not to Touch the Earth

Words & Music by The Doors

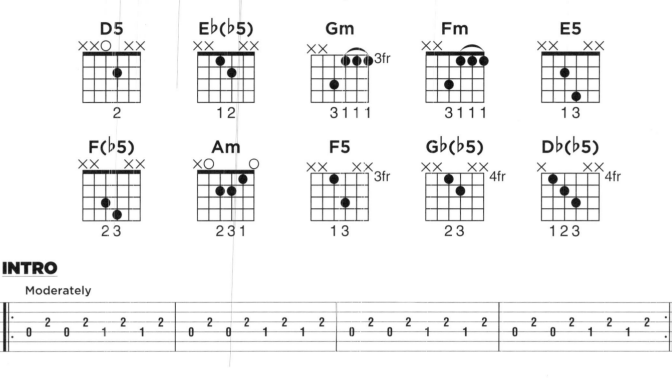

INTRO

Moderately

VERSE 1

D5   **Eb(b5)** **D5**   **Eb(b5)** **D5**   **Eb(b5)** **D5**   **Eb(b5)**
Not to touch the earth,   not to see the sun,   nothing left to do   but run, run, run, let's run.

D5 **Eb(b5)** **D5** **Eb(b5)**   **D5** **Eb(b5)** **D5** **Eb(b5)**
                Let's run.

D5   **Eb(b5)** **D5**   **Eb(b5)** **D5**   **Eb(b5)** **D5**   **Eb(b5)**
House up on the hill,   moon is lying still,   shadows of the trees   witnessing the wild breeze,

D5   **Eb(b5)** **D5** **Eb(b5)**   **D5** **N.C.**
come on, baby, run with me.   Let's run.

CHORUS 1

Gm   **Fm**
Run with me, run with me.

Gm   **D5** **N.C.**
Run with me, let's run.

INTERLUDE

The

VERSE 2

E5	F(♭5)	E5	F(♭5)	E5	F(♭5)	E5	F(♭5)

mansion is warm at the top of the hill.   Rich are the rooms and the comforts there.

E5	F(♭5)	E5	F(♭5)	E5	F(♭5)	E5	F(♭5)

Red are the arms of luxuriant chairs.   And you won't know a thing 'till you get inside.

E5 F(♭5) E5 F(♭5) E5 F(♭5) E5 F(♭5)

E5	F(♭5)	E5	F(♭5)	E5	F(♭5)	E5	F(♭5)

Dead president's corpse in the driver's car,   the engine runs on   glue and tar.

E5	F(♭5)	E5	F(♭5)	E5	F(♭5)	E5	F(♭5) E5 N.C.

Come on along, not going very far;   to the east,   to meet the Czar.

CHORUS 2

Am   Gm
Run with me, run with me.

Am   E5 N.C.
Run with me, let's run.

INTERLUDE

Whoa!   Some

VERSE 2

F5	G♭(♭5)	F5	G♭(♭5)	F5	G♭(♭5)	F5	G♭(♭5)

outlaws live by the side of the lake;   the minister's daughter's in love with a snake

F5	G♭(♭5)	F5	G♭(♭5)	F5	G♭(♭5)	F5	G♭(♭5)

who lives in a well by the side of the road.   Wake up, girl,   we're almost home.

F5 G♭(♭5) F5 G♭(♭5) F5 G♭(♭5) F5 G♭(♭5)
Yeah, c'mon!

F5   G♭(♭5)   F5   G♭(♭5)
  We should see   the gates   by morning.

F5 G♭(♭5) F5 G♭(♭5) F5 G♭(♭5) F5 G♭(♭5)

F5   G♭(♭5) F5   G♭(♭5) F5 G♭(♭5) F5 G♭(♭5)
  We should be   inside by evening.

F5   G♭(♭5)   F5 G♭(♭5) F5 G♭(♭5)
Sun, sun, sun.

F5   G♭(♭5) F5 G♭(♭5) F5   G♭(♭5) F5 G♭(♭5)
Burn, burn, burn.   Soon, soon, soon.

F5 G♭(♭5) F5   G♭(♭5) F5 G♭(♭5)   F5 G♭(♭5)
Moon, moon, moon.   I   will get you

F5 G♭(♭5) F5 G♭(♭5) F5   G♭(♭5) F5 G♭(♭5) F5   G♭(♭5) F5 G♭(♭5)
  soon,   soon,   soon.

F5 G♭(♭5) F5 D♭(♭5) F5
           Spoken: I am the Lizard King, I can do anything.

Peace Frog

(Morrison/Krieger)

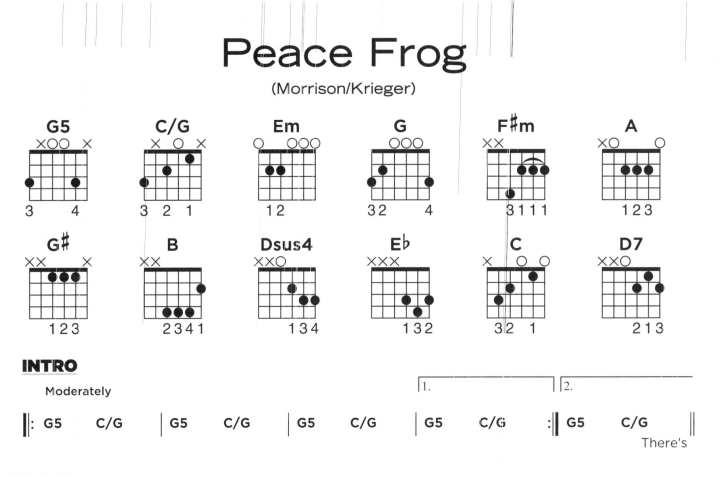

INTRO

Moderately

‖: G5   C/G | G5   C/G | G5   C/G | G5   C/G :‖ G5   C/G ‖

1.   2.

There's

VERSE 1

G5   C/G   G5 C/G   G5   C/G   G5 C/G
blood in the streets, it's up to my ankles.   Blood in the streets, it's up to my knee.
                                                     (She came.)

G5   C/G   G5 C/G   G5   C/G   G5 C/G
Blood in the streets, the town of Chicago.   Blood on the rise is following me.
(She came.)   *(She came.)*

G5   C/G   G5   C/G
Just about the break of day.

CHORUS 1

Em   G   F♯m   A N.C.
She came and then she drove away, sunlight in her hair.

VERSE 2

G5   C/G   G5 C/G
Blood in the streets, runs a river of sadness.
(She came.)

G5   C/G   G5 C/G
Blood in the streets, it's up to my thigh.
(She came.)

G5   C/G   G5 C/G
Yeah, the river runs red down the legs of the city.
(She came.)

G5   C/G   G5 C/G
The women are cryin', the rivers are weepin'.
(She came.)

CHORUS 2

Em   G   F#m   A   G#   B

She came in town and then she drove away, sunlight in her hair.

INTERLUDE 1

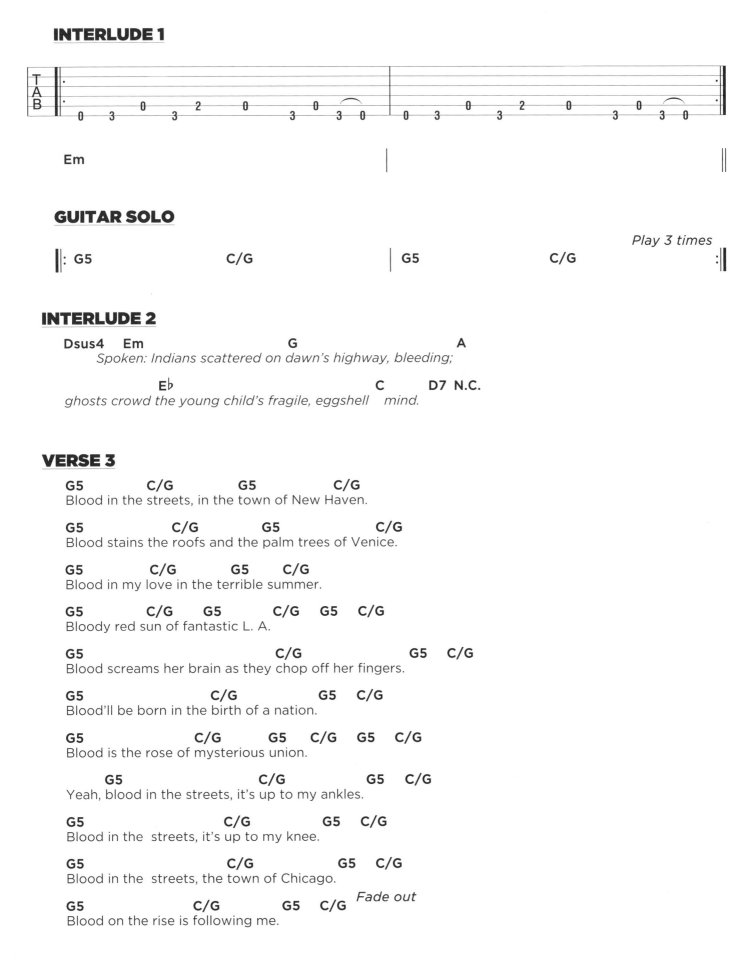

Em

GUITAR SOLO

Play 3 times

‖: G5   C/G | G5   C/G   :‖

INTERLUDE 2

Dsus4   Em   G   A

Spoken: Indians scattered on dawn's highway, bleeding;

                     E♭   C   D7 N.C.

ghosts crowd the young child's fragile, eggshell   mind.

VERSE 3

G5   C/G   G5   C/G

Blood in the streets, in the town of New Haven.

G5   C/G   G5   C/G

Blood stains the roofs and the palm trees of Venice.

G5   C/G   G5   C/G

Blood in my love in the terrible summer.

G5   C/G   G5   C/G G5 C/G

Bloody red sun of fantastic L. A.

G5   C/G   G5   C/G

Blood screams her brain as they chop off her fingers.

G5   C/G   G5 C/G

Blood'll be born in the birth of a nation.

G5   C/G   G5 C/G G5 C/G

Blood is the rose of mysterious union.

     G5   C/G   G5 C/G

Yeah, blood in the streets, it's up to my ankles.

G5   C/G   G5 C/G

Blood in the streets, it's up to my knee.

G5   C/G   G5 C/G

Blood in the streets, the town of Chicago.

G5   C/G   G5 C/G   *Fade out*

Blood on the rise is following me.

People Are Strange

Words & Music by The Doors

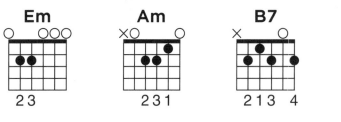
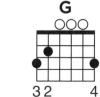

INTRO

Moderately

```
T|----------------------------------|
A|----------------------------------|
B|---2--------0---------------------|
|------------------3---------------|
```

VERSE 1

Em   Am   Em Am   Em B7   Em
People are strange when you're a stranger, faces look ugly when you're alone.

          Am   Em Am   Em B7   Em
Women seem wicked when you're unwanted, streets seem un - even when you're down.

CHORUS 1

        B7 G   B7
When you're strange, faces come of the rain.

             G   B7
When you're strange,   no one remembers your name.

When you're strange, when you're strange, when you're strange. *(Alright, yeah.)

                         *2nd time only

REPEAT VERSE 1

GUITAR SOLO

                    1.   2.

‖: B7 | | Em | :‖ N.C

REPEAT CHORUS 1

PIANO SOLO

                    1.   2.

‖: Em | Am Em | Am Em | B7 Em :‖ B7 Em

CHORUS 2

```
            B7        G                     B7
When you're strange, faces come of the rain.

                      G                           B7
When you're strange, no one remembers your name.

                                              N.C.         B7
When you're strange, when you're strange, when you're      strange.
```

Riders on the Storm

Words & Music by The Doors

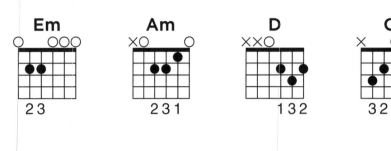

INTRODUCTION

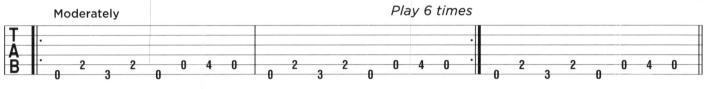

INTRO

Moderately

Play 6 times

VERSE 1

Em
Riders on the storm, riders on the storm.

Am   **Em**
Into this house we're born, into this world we're thrown.

D   **C**   **Em**
Like a dog without a bone, an actor out on loan. Riders on the storm.

VERSE 2

Em
There's a killer on the road; his brain is squirming like a toad.

Am   **Em**
Take a long holiday; let your children play.

D   **C**   **Em**
If you give this man a ride, sweet family will die. Killer on the road. Yeah.

GUITAR SOLO

Girl, you

VERSE 3

Em
gotta love your man. Girl, you gotta love your man.

Am   **Em**
Take him by the hand; make him understand.

   D   **C**   **Em**
The world on you depends, our life will never end. Gotta love your man. Yeah.

ELECTRIC PIANO SOLO

Play 12 times

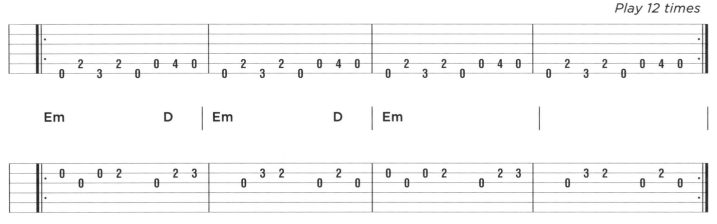

Em   D   Em   D   Em

REPEAT VERSE 1

OUTRO

Rid - ers on the storm.   Rid - ers on the storm.

Repeat and fade

Roadhouse Blues

(Morrison/Doors)

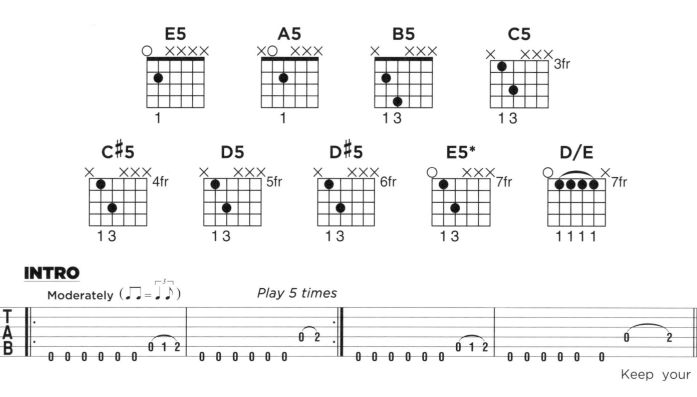

INTRO

Moderately

Play 5 times

Keep your

VERSE 1

E5
eyes on the road, your hand upon the wheel.

Keep your eyes on the road, your hand upon the wheel.

Yeah, we're goin' to the roadhouse, gonna have a real, a good time.

VERSE 2

E5
Yeah, the back of the roadhouse they got some bungalows.

Yeah, the back of the roadhouse they got some bungalows.

And that's for the people like to go down slow.

CHORUS 1

A5
Let it roll, baby, roll. Let it roll, baby, roll.

B5   C5   B5
Let it roll, baby, roll. Let it roll,   all   night

GUITAR SOLO

Play 7 times

| E5 | | |: | :| | :| |

long. *Spoken: Do it, Robby, do it.*   You gotta

VERSE 3

E5
roll, roll, roll, you gotta thrill my soul, alright.

Roll, roll, roll, roll a-through my soul, da-gotta-peepa-konja-chu-cha. Ho-conk-conk-a-donta.

Eat-cha-coon-an-eat-cha. Bop-a-lula-eat-cha. Bomp-a-kee-chow. Ee-sonk-conk, yeah, right.

VERSE 4

E5
Ashen lady, ashen lady,

give up your vows, give up your vows.

Save our city, save our city right now.

VERSE 5

E5
Well, I woke up this morning, I got myself a beer.

Yeah, I woke up this morning and I got myself a beer.

The future's uncertain and the end is always near.

CHORUS 2

A5
Let it roll, baby, roll. Let it roll, baby, roll.

B5　　**C5 C♯5 D5**　　**D♯5 E5 N.C. E5* D/E**
Let it roll, baby, roll. Let it roll, hey,　　all　　night

Ship of Fools

(Morrison/Krieger)

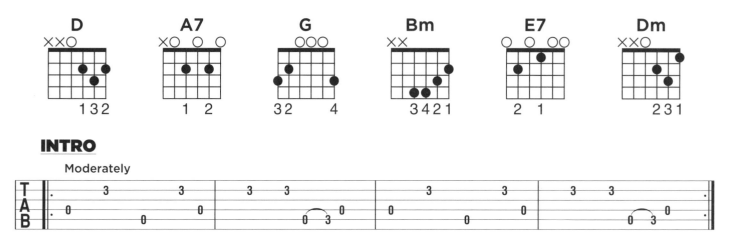

INTRO

Moderately

VERSE 1

D
The human race was dying out,

A7
no one left to scream and shout.

D   G   Bm
People walking on the moon,

E7   A7
smog will get you pretty soon.

VERSE 2

D
Everyone was hanging out,

A7
hanging up and hanging down.

D   G   Bm
Hanging in and holding fast,

E7   A7   D
hope our little world will last.

INTERLUDE

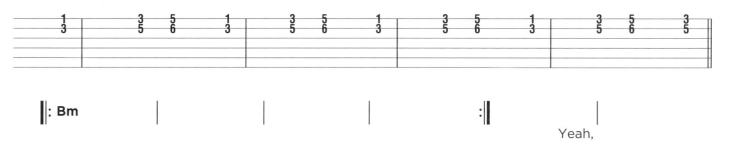

Yeah,

BRIDGE

Bm
along came mister good trips, looking for a new ship.

Come on, people, better climb on board.

Come on, baby, now we're going home.

Ship of fools. Ship of fools.

GUITAR SOLO

Play 4 times

‖: **Dm**　　　　　　　|　　　　　　　:‖ **G**　　**Bm**　|　**E7**　　**A7**　　‖

VERSE 2

D
The human race was dying out,

　　　　　　　　　　　　　A7
no one left to scream and shout.

D　　　　　　　　　　**G Bm**
People walking on the moon,

E7　　　　　　　**A7**
smog gonn' get you pretty soon.

OUTRO

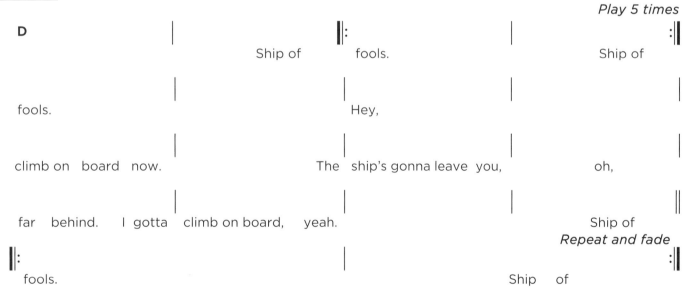

Play 5 times

D　　　　　　　|　　‖:　　　　　　|　　　　　　:‖
　　　　　　　　　　Ship of　　fools.　　　　　　　Ship of

|　　　　　　　|　　　　　　|　　　　　|
fools.　　　　　　　　　　Hey,

|　　　　　　　|　　　　　　|　　　　　|
climb on　board　now.　　　　The　ship's gonna leave　you,　　　oh,

|　　　　　　　|　　　　　　|　　　　　‖
far　behind.　I　gotta　climb on board,　yeah.　　　　　Ship of

Repeat and fade

‖:　　　　　　　|　　　　　　　　　　　　　　:‖
fools.　　　　　　　　　　　Ship　of

37

Soul Kitchen

Words & Music by The Doors

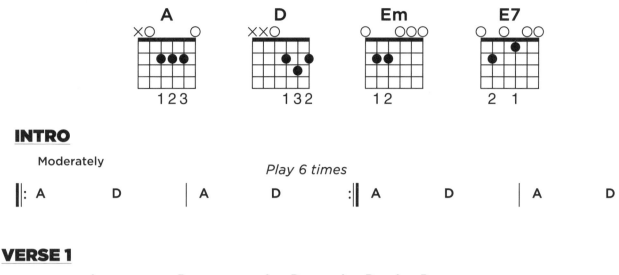

INTRO

Moderately

Play 6 times

‖: A | D | A | D   :‖ A | D | A | D

VERSE 1

       A   D   A   D   A D A D
Well, the clock says it's time to close   now.

   A   D   A   D   A D A D
I guess I'd better go   now.

       A   D   A   D   A D A D
I'd really like to stay   here all night.

       A   D   A   D   A   D   A   D
The cars crawl past all stuffed with eyes,   street lights shed their hollow glow.

       A   D   A   D   D   A   D
Your brain seems bruised with numb surprise.   Still one place to go,

  A   D   A   D
still one place to go.

CHORUS

      Em   D   Em   D   Em   D   Em   D
Let me sleep all night   in your   soul kitchen,   warm my mind near your   gentle stove.

Em   D   Em   D   E7
    Turn me out and I'll wander, baby, stumbling in the neon groves.

VERSE 2

       A   D   A   D   A   D   A   D
Well, your fingers weave quick minarets,   speaking secret alphabets.

  A   D   A   D   A   D   A   D   A   A   D
I light another cigarette,   learn to forget,   learn to forget,

  A   D   A   D   A   D   A   D
learn to forget,   learn to forget.

REPEAT CHORUS

GUITAR SOLO

Play 4 times

‖: A   D | A   D | A   D | A   D   :‖

INTERLUDE

A   D | A   D | A   D | A   D

VERSE 3

```
          A        D        A  D    A D A D
Well, the clock says it's time to close      now.

   A    D      A   D    A D A D
I know I have to go      now.

   A   D      A    D     A D A D      A D A D      A
I really want to stay  here all night,         all night,        all night.
```

Spanish Caravan

Words & Music by The Doors

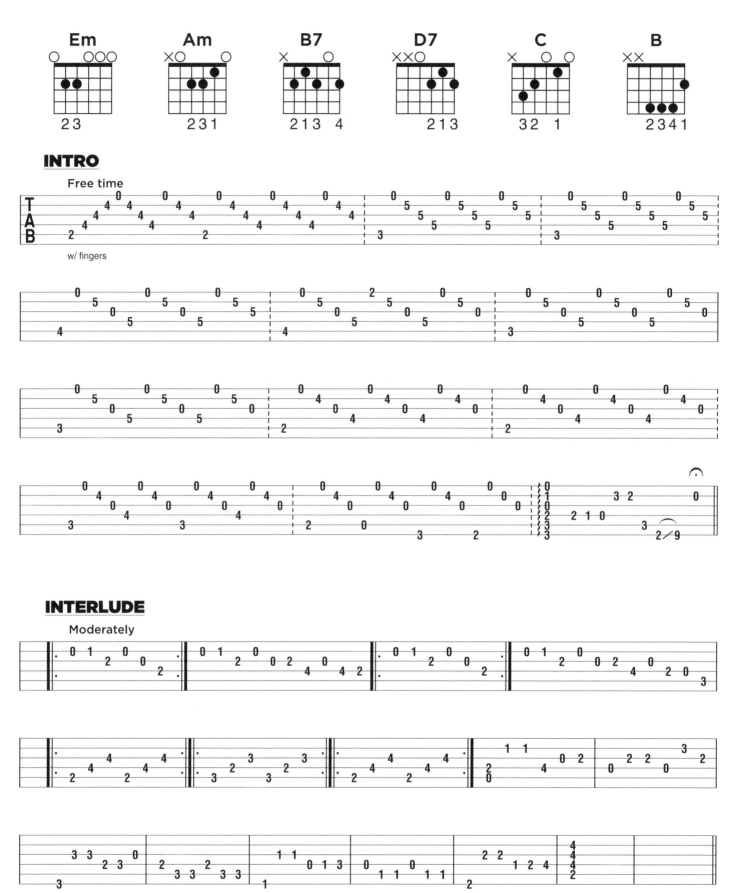

VERSE 1

Em   Am   B7   Em
Carry me, caravan, take me away.

             Am   B7   Em
Take me to Portugal, take me to Spain.

Am   Em   B7   Em
Andalusia, with fields full of grain.

Am   Em   B7   Em
I have to see you again and again.

                   D7   C   B
Take me Spanish caravan,   yes, I know you can.

REPEAT INTERLUDE

VERSE 2

Em   Am   B7   Em
Trade winds find galleons lost in the sea.

           Am   B7   Em
I know where treasure is waiting for me.

Am   Em   B7   Em
Silver and gold and the mountains of Spain;

Am   Em   B7   Em
I have to see you again and again.

                   D7   C   B7
Take me Spanish caravan,   yes, I know you can.

Touch Me

(Krieger)

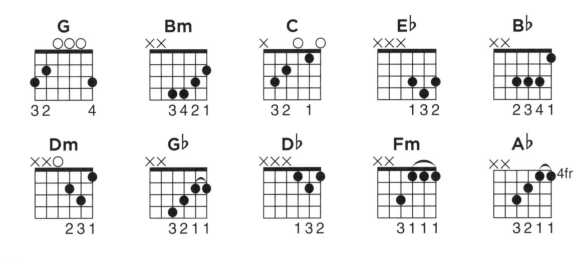

INTRO

Moderately

Play 7 times

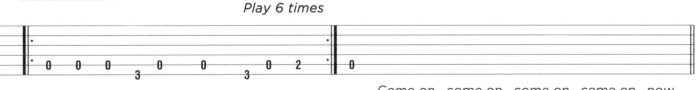

Come on, come on, come on, come on, now,

VERSE 1

G   Bm   C   Eb

touch me, babe.   Can't you see that I am not afraid?

               Bb   Dm   Eb   Gb

What was that promise that you made?   Why won't you tell what she said?

               Db

What was that promise that you made?

CHORUS 1

       Gb   Fm   Gb   Ab   Db

Now, I'm gonna love you 'til the heavens stop the rain.

Gb   Fm   Gb   Ab   Gb   Db

I'm gonna love you 'til the stars fall   from the sky for you and I.

INTERLUDE

Play 6 times

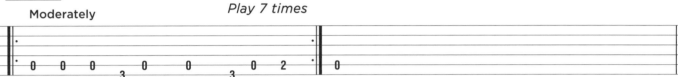

Come on, come on, come on, come on, now,

REPEAT VERSE 1

REPEAT CHORUS 1

CHORUS 2

Gb   Fm   Gb   Ab   Db
I'm gonna love you 'til the heavens stop the rain.

Gb   Fm   Gb   Ab   Gb   Db
I'm gonna love you 'til the stars fall from the sky for you and I.

INTERLUDE 2

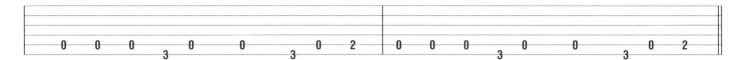

SAX SOLO

Play 9 times

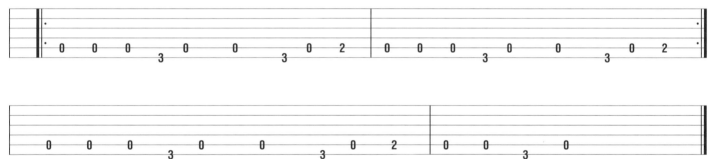

Waiting for the Sun

(Morrison)

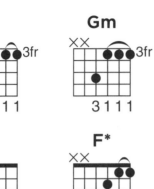
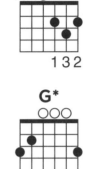
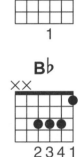

INTRO

Moderately

| D7 | | G | | Gm | | D |

VERSE 1

D7   G   Gm   D5 F D5 F
At first flash of Eden we race down to the sea,

D7   G   Gm   D5 F D5 F D5 F D5 F
standing there on freedom's shore.

CHORUS 1

E♭   F* G* E♭   F* G* E♭   F*   D
Waiting for the sun, waiting for the sun, waiting for the sun.

VERSE 2

D7   G Gm   D5 F D5 F
  Can't you feel it, now that spring has come;

       D7   G   Gm   D5 F D5 F D5 F
that it's time to live in the   scattered sun?

CHORUS 2

E♭   F* G* E♭   F* G*
Waiting for the sun, waiting for the sun,

E♭   F* D E♭   F* G*
waiting for the sun, waiting for the sun.

BRIDGE

Gm   B♭   F*   Gm
Waiting, waiting, waiting, waiting.

           B♭   F*   Gm
Waiting, waiting, waiting, waiting.

                  F*   Gm
Waiting for you to   come along.

                  F*   Gm
Waiting for you to   hear my song.

                  F*   Gm
Waiting for you to   come along.

                  F*   Gm
Waiting for you to tell me what went wrong.

           F*   E♭   D   Gm
This is the strangest life I've ever known, yeah!

INTERLUDE

‖: D5   F   D5 F | D5   F   D5 F | D5   F   D5 F | D5   F   D5 F   :‖

VERSE 3

D7   G   Gm   D
   Can't you feel it, now that spring has come;

        D7   G   Gm   D5 F D5 F D5 F D5 F
that it's   time to live in the   scattered sun?

CHORUS 3

E♭   F*   G*   E♭   F*   G*
Waiting for the sun, waiting for the sun,

E♭   F*   D   E♭   F*   G*
waiting for the sun, waiting for the sun.

OUTRO

D5   F   D5   F | D5   F   D5   F   N.C.   ‖

Wild Child

(Morrison)

(Capo 3rd Fret)

INTRO

Moderately

Play 3 times

```
T |:--------0-----------------------|----------0-----------------:|
A |: 2---2--------2--2--2--2--0------| 2---2---------2--2--2--2--0-:|
B |:------------------------------2-|--------------------------2-:|
```

VERSE 1

Em   G   Em   G   Em
Wild   child,   full of grace,

   G   Em   G   Em
savior of the human race.

    G   Em F# F
Your cool face.

```
|-----2-0---2-0---2-0---2-0-------|------0------------------------|------0------------------------|
|-------2-----2-----2-----2-------| 2--2-----2--2--2--2-0---------| 2--2-----2--2--2--2-0---------|
|---------------------------------|-------------------------2-----|-------------------------2-----|
```

VERSE 2

Em   G   Em   G   Em
Natural child, terrible child,

   G   Em   G   Em
not your mother's or your father's child.

    G   Em   G   Em F# F
You're our child, screamin' wild.

```
|-----2-0---2-0---2-0---2-0-------|------0------------------------|------0------------------------|
|-------2-----2-----2-----2-------| 2--2-----2--2--2--2-0---------| 2--2-----2--2--2--2-0---------|
|---------------------------------|-------------------------2-----|-------------------------2-----|
```

INTERLUDE

| A7 | | | Em | | | | | |
| E | |

A7 | | Em | |

A7 | | E |

BRIDGE

      G   A   G   A
With hunger at her heels, freedom in her eyes, she dances on her knees, pirate prince at her

G   F#   F   Em N.C.   Em
  side,   staring   into   the hollow idol's eyes.

OUTRO

Em
      Wild child, full of grace, savior of the human race.

      Your cool face, your cool face, your cool face.

Spoken: Do you remember when we were in Africa?

REALLY EASY GUITAR

Easy-to-follow charts to get you playing right away are presented in these collections of arrangements in chords, lyrics and basic tab for all guitarists.

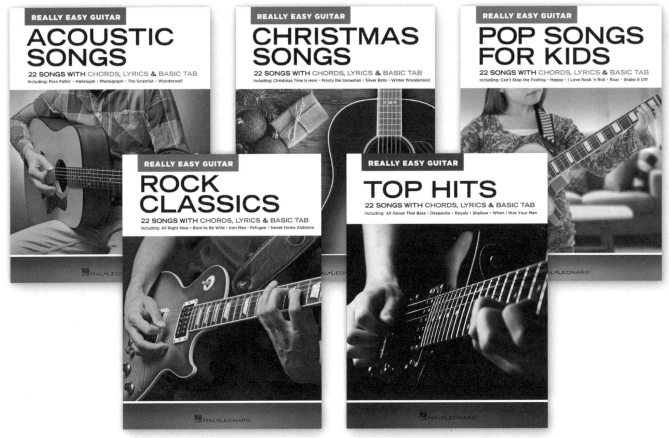

ACOUSTIC CLASSICS
22 songs: Angie • Best of My Love • Dust in the Wind • Fire and Rain • A Horse with No Name • Layla • More Than a Feeling • Night Moves • Patience • Time in a Bottle • Wanted Dead or Alive • and more.
00300600 ....$9.99

ACOUSTIC SONGS
22 songs: Free Fallin' • Good Riddance (Time of Your Life) • Hallelujah • I'm Yours • Losing My Religion • Mr. Jones • Photograph • Riptide • The Scientist • Wonderwall • and more.
00286663 ....$9.99

THE BEATLES FOR KIDS
14 songs: All You Need Is Love • Blackbird • Good Day Sunshine • Here Comes the Sun • I Want to Hold Your Hand • Let It Be • With a Little Help from My Friends • Yellow Submarine • and more.
00346031..$9.99

CHRISTMAS CLASSICS
22 Christmas carols: Away in a Manger • Deck the Hall • It Came upon the Midnight Clear • Jingle Bells • Silent Night • The Twelve Days of Christmas • We Wish You a Merry Christmas • and more.
00348327..$9.99

CHRISTMAS SONGS
22 holiday favorites: Blue Christmas • Christmas Time Is Here • Frosty the Snowman • Have Yourself a Merry Little Christmas • Mary, Did You Know? • Silver Bells • Winter Wonderland • and more.
00294775 ....$9.99

THE DOORS
22 songs: Break on Through to the Other Side • Hello, I Love You (Won't You Tell Me Your Name?) • L.A. Woman • Light My Fire • Love Her Madly • People Are Strange • Riders on the Storm • Touch Me • and more.
00345890 ....$9.99

BILLIE EILISH
14 songs: All the Good Girls Go to Hell • Bad Guy • Everything I Wanted • Idontwannabeyouanymore • No Time to Die • Ocean Eyes • Six Feet Under • Wish You Were Gay • and more.
00346351 ....$9.99

POP SONGS FOR KIDS
22 songs: Brave • Can't Stop the Feeling • Happy • I Love Rock 'N Roll • Let It Go • Roar • Shake It Off • We Got the Beat • and more.
00286698 ....$9.99

ROCK CLASSICS
22 songs: All Right Now • Born to Be Wild • Don't Fear the Reaper • Hey Joe • Iron Man • Old Time Rock & Roll • Refugee • Sweet Home Alabama • You Shook Me All Night Long • and more.
00286699 ....$9.99

TOP HITS
22 hits: All About That Bass • All of Me • Despacito • Love Yourself • Royals • Say Something • Shallow • Someone like You • This Is Me • A Thousand Years • When I Was Your Man • and more.
00300599..$9.99

halleonard.com